This Coloring Book

belongs to

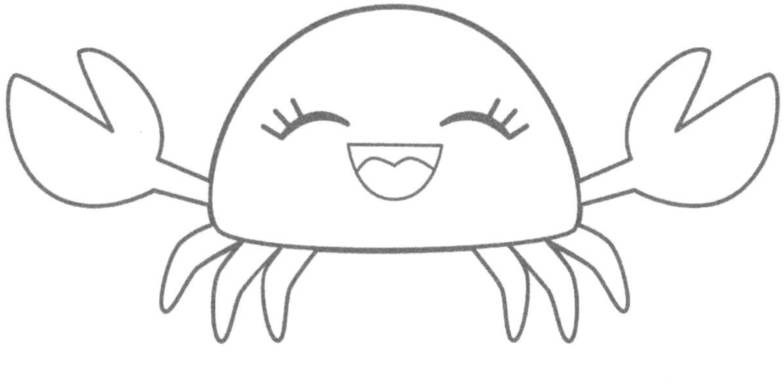

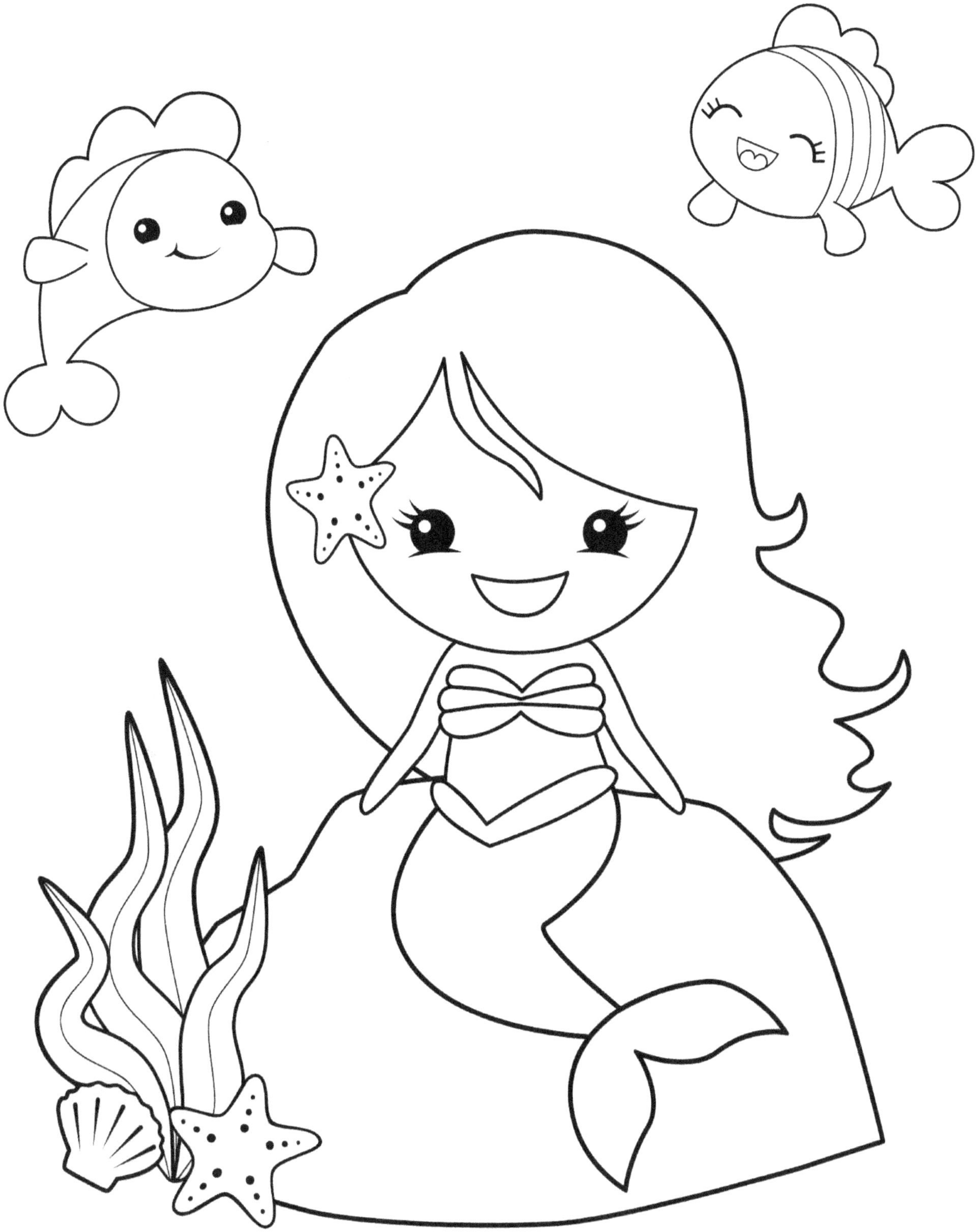

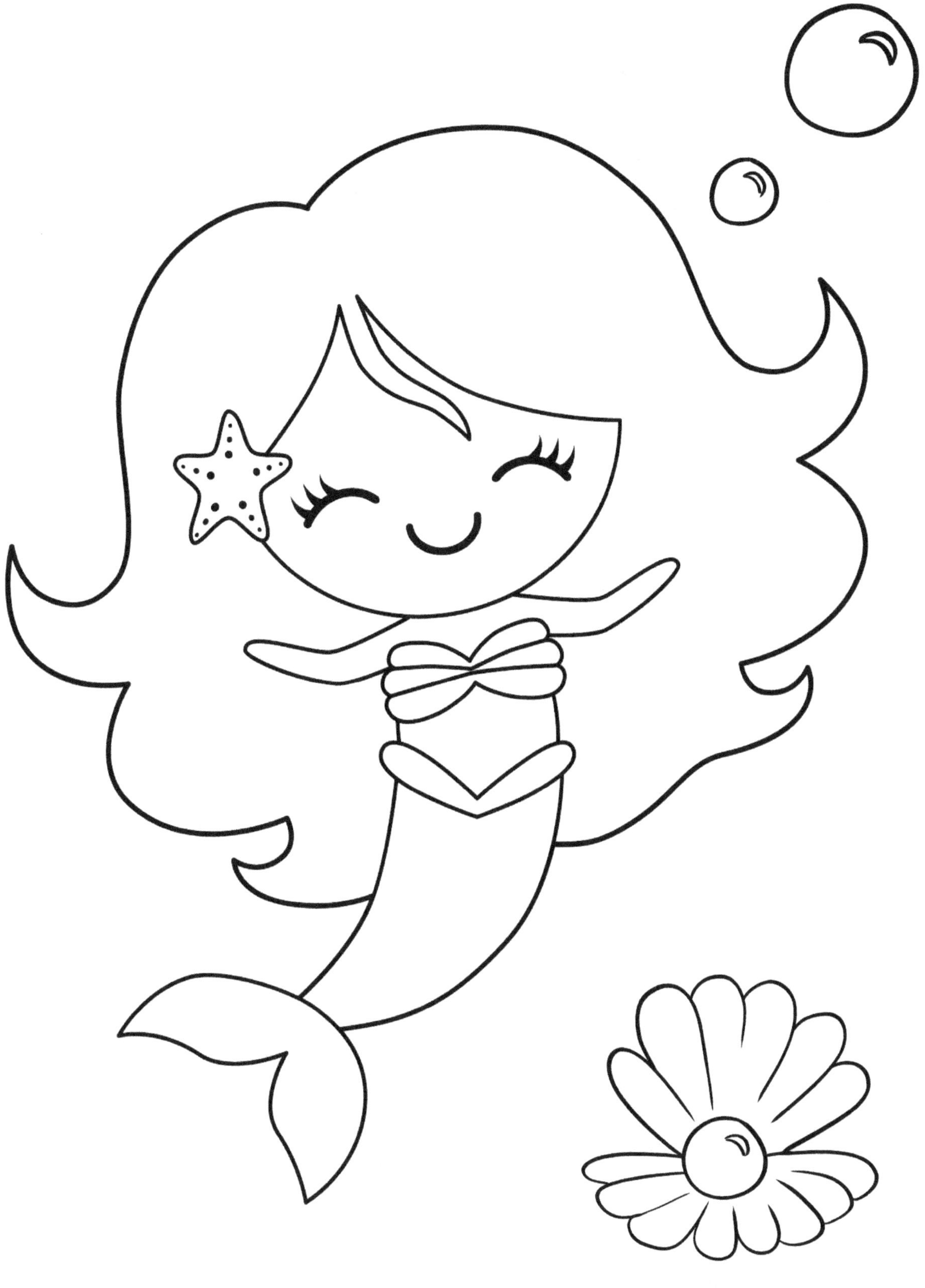

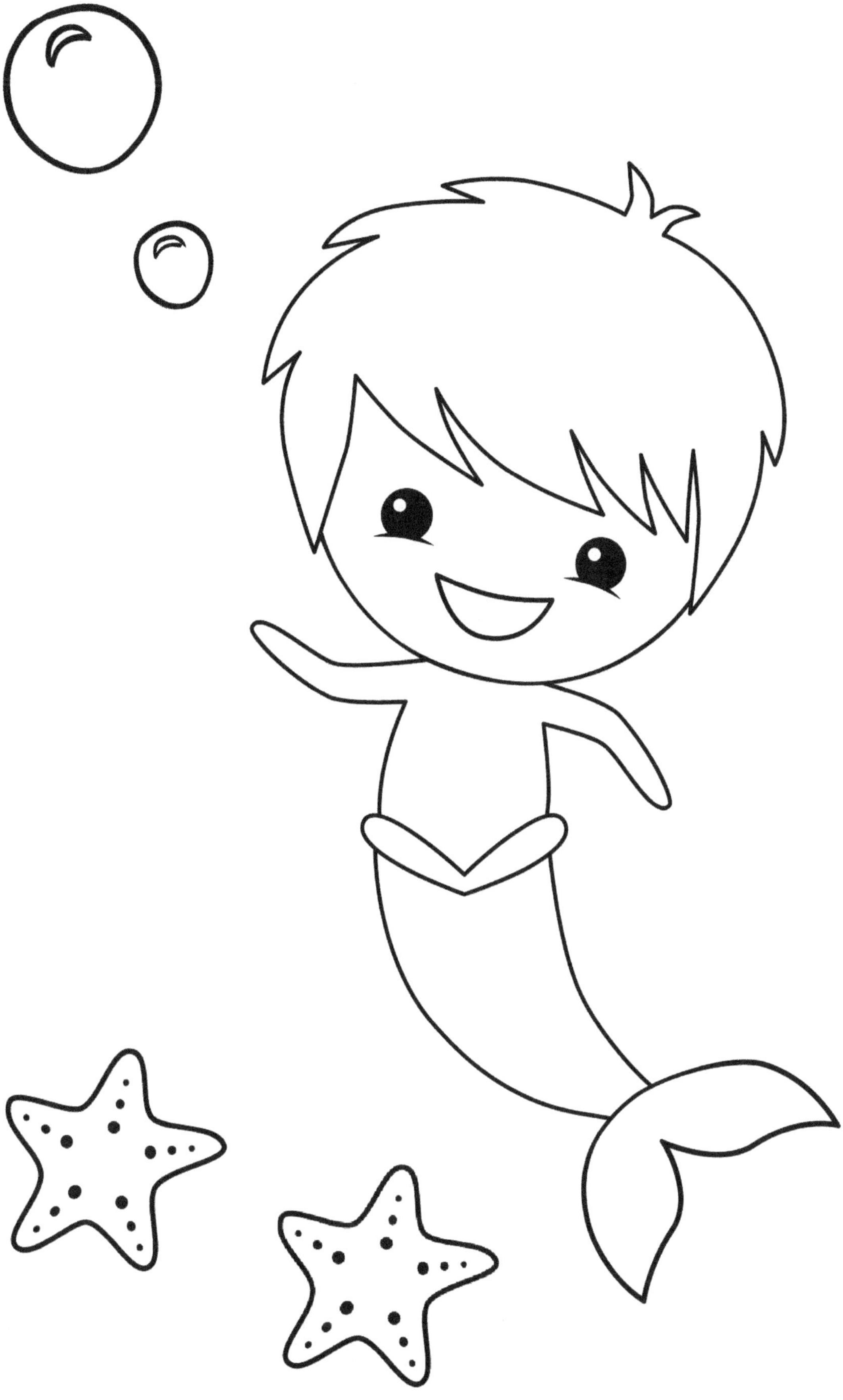

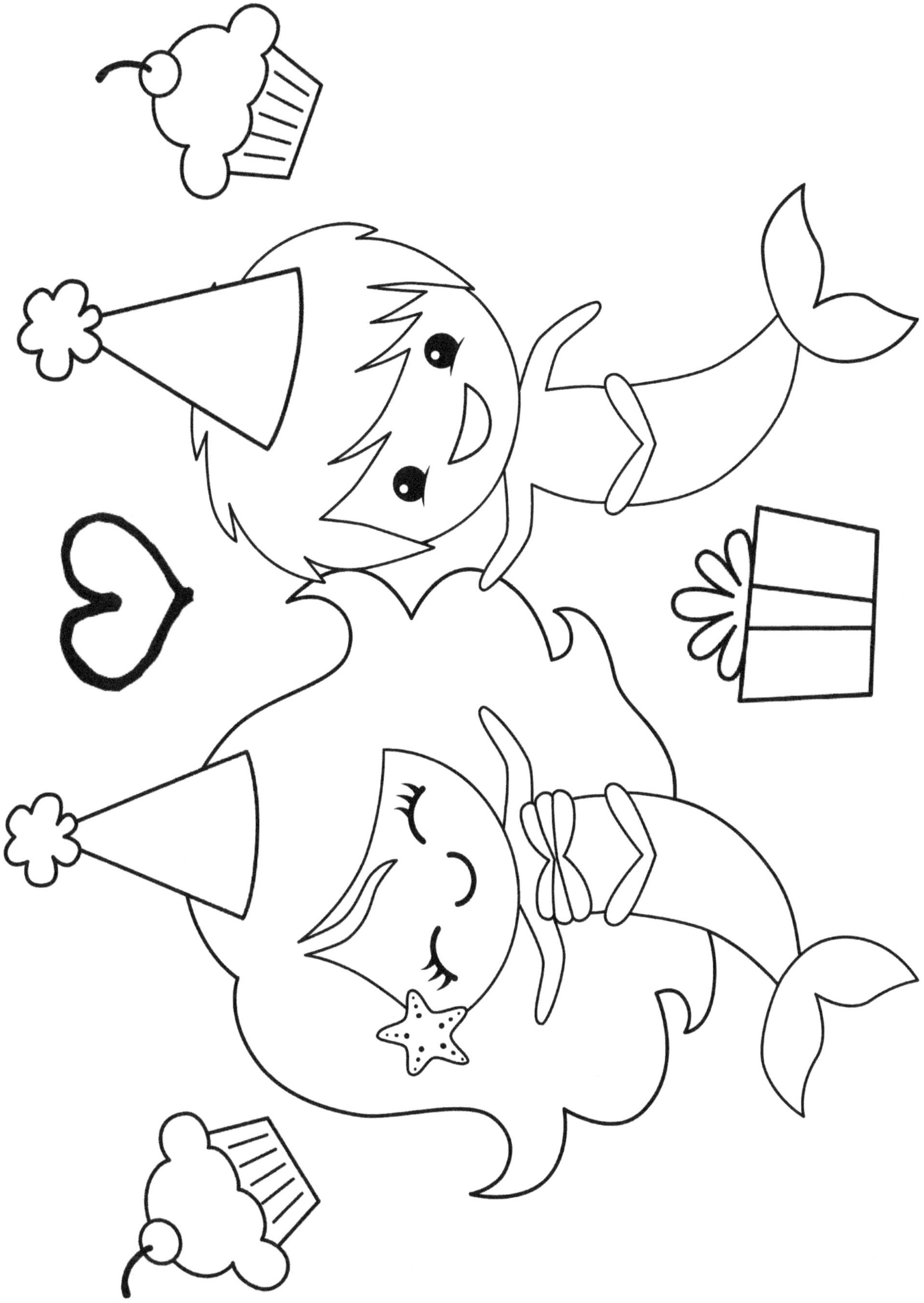

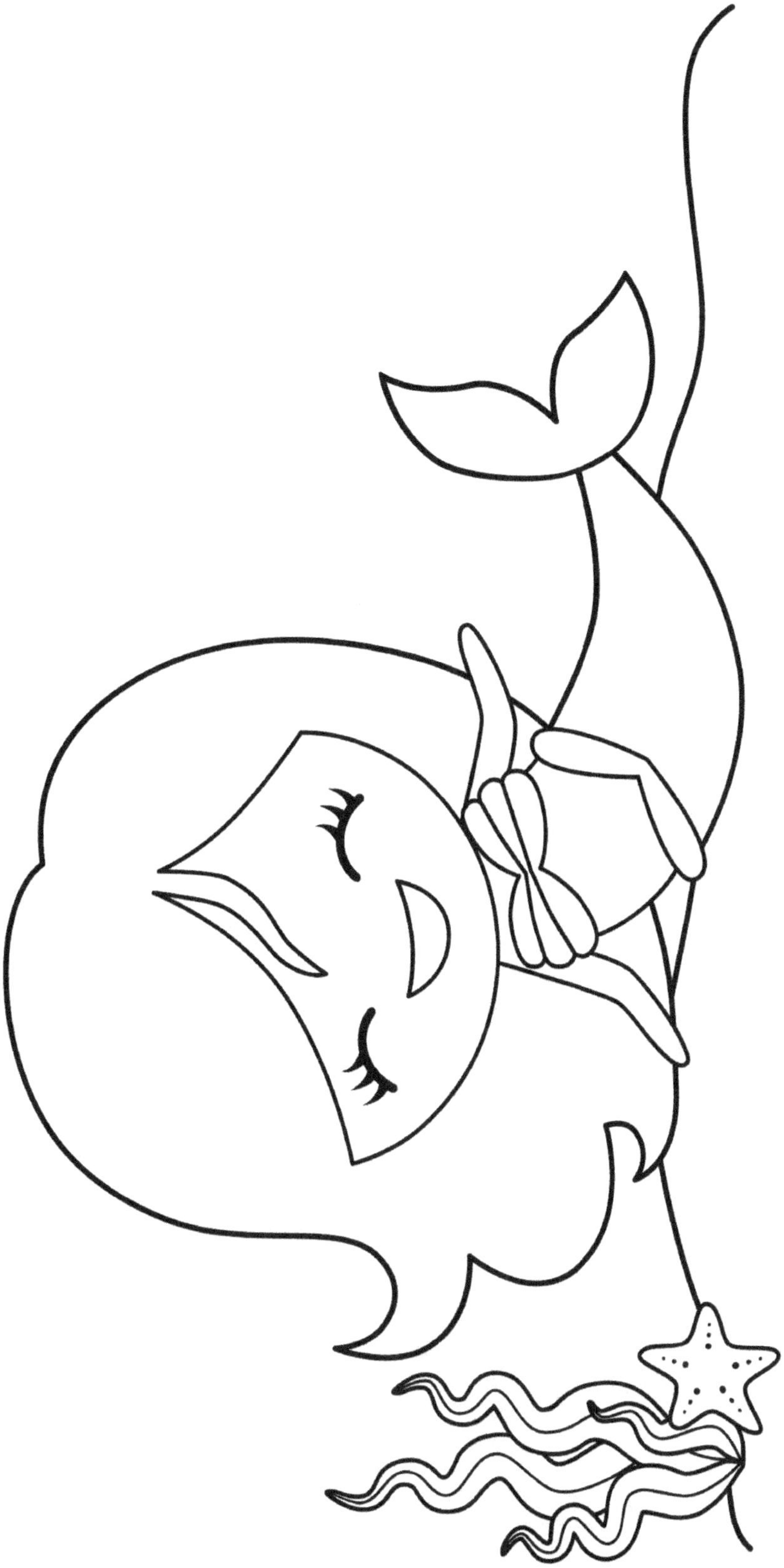

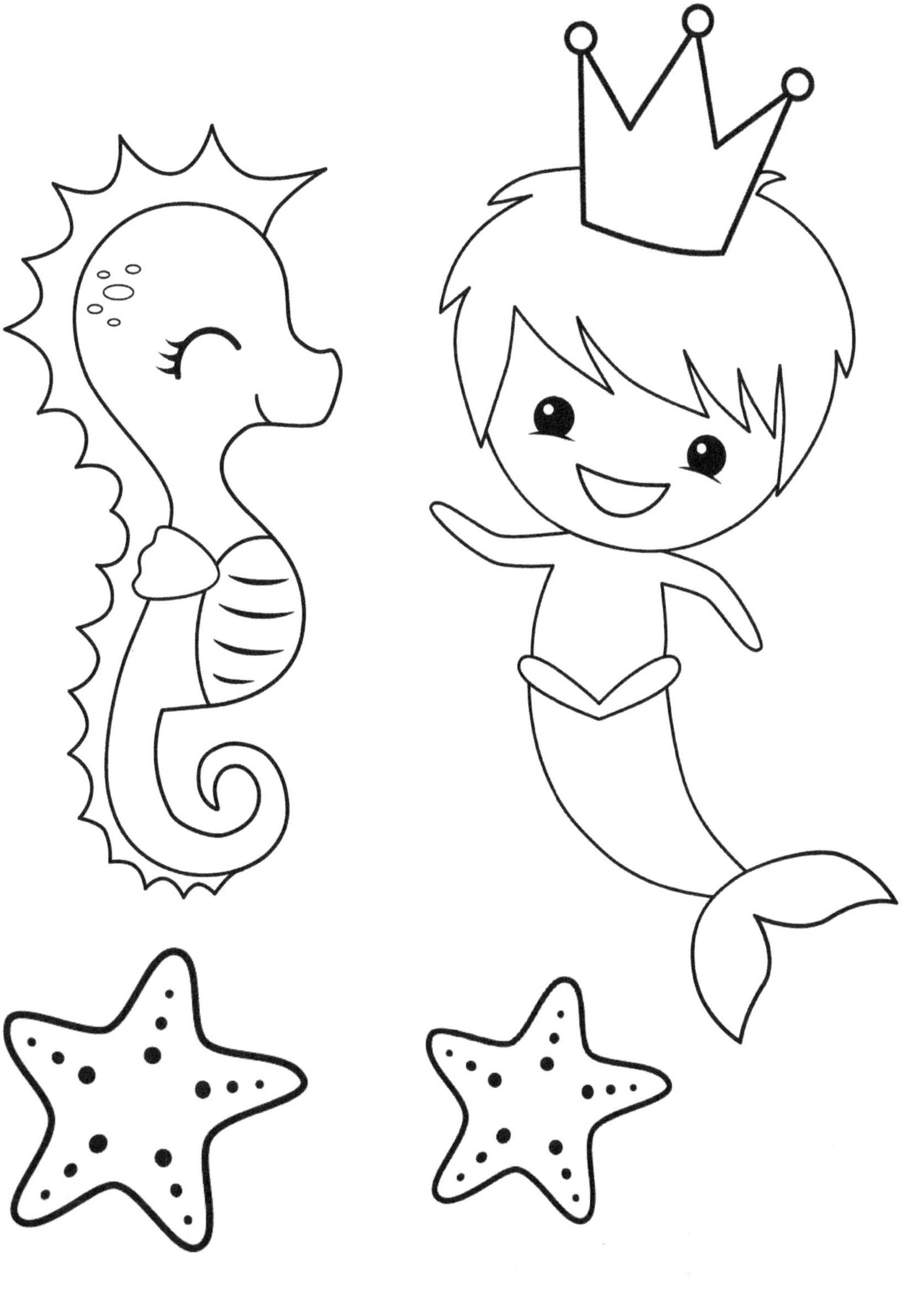

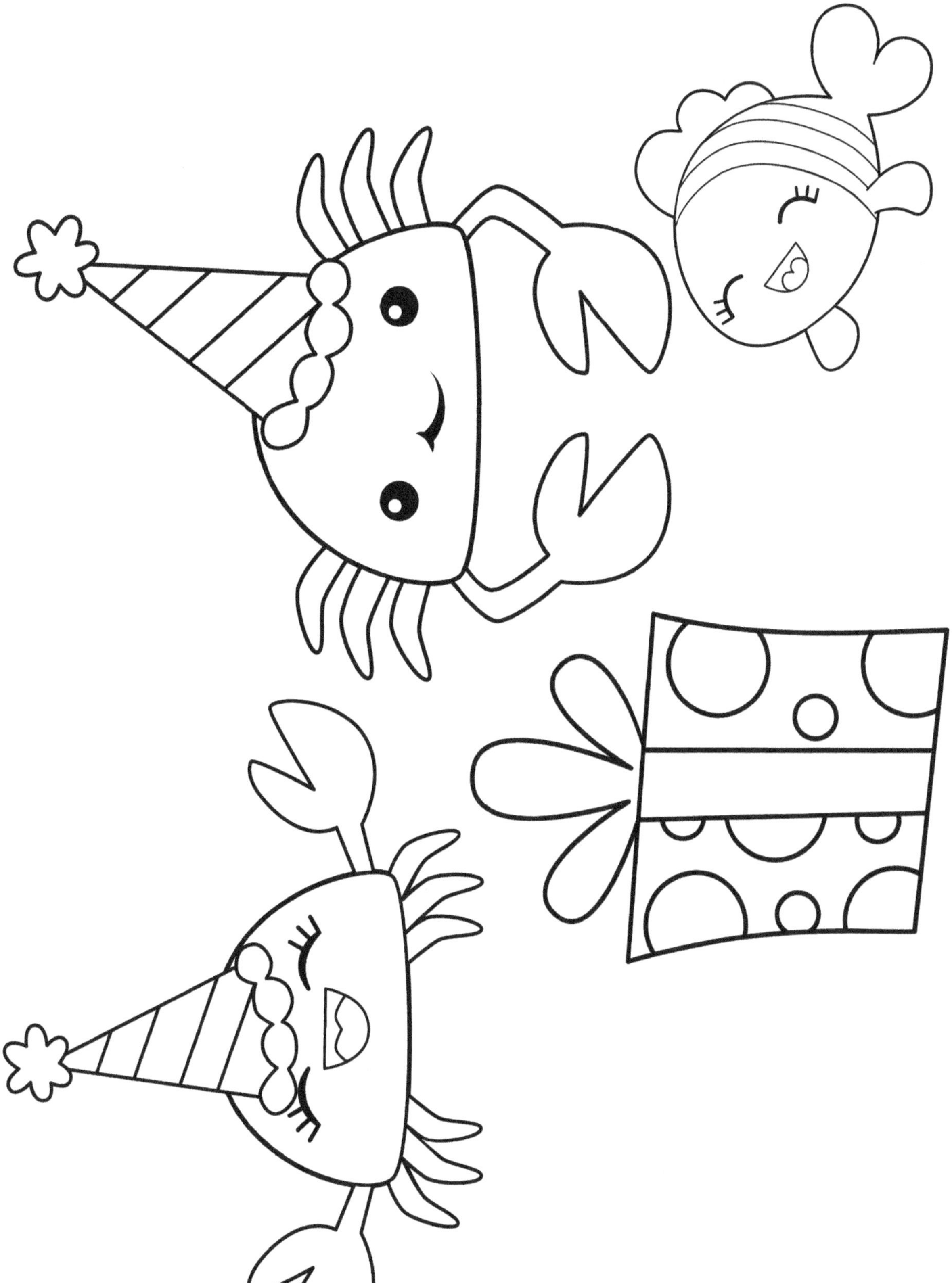

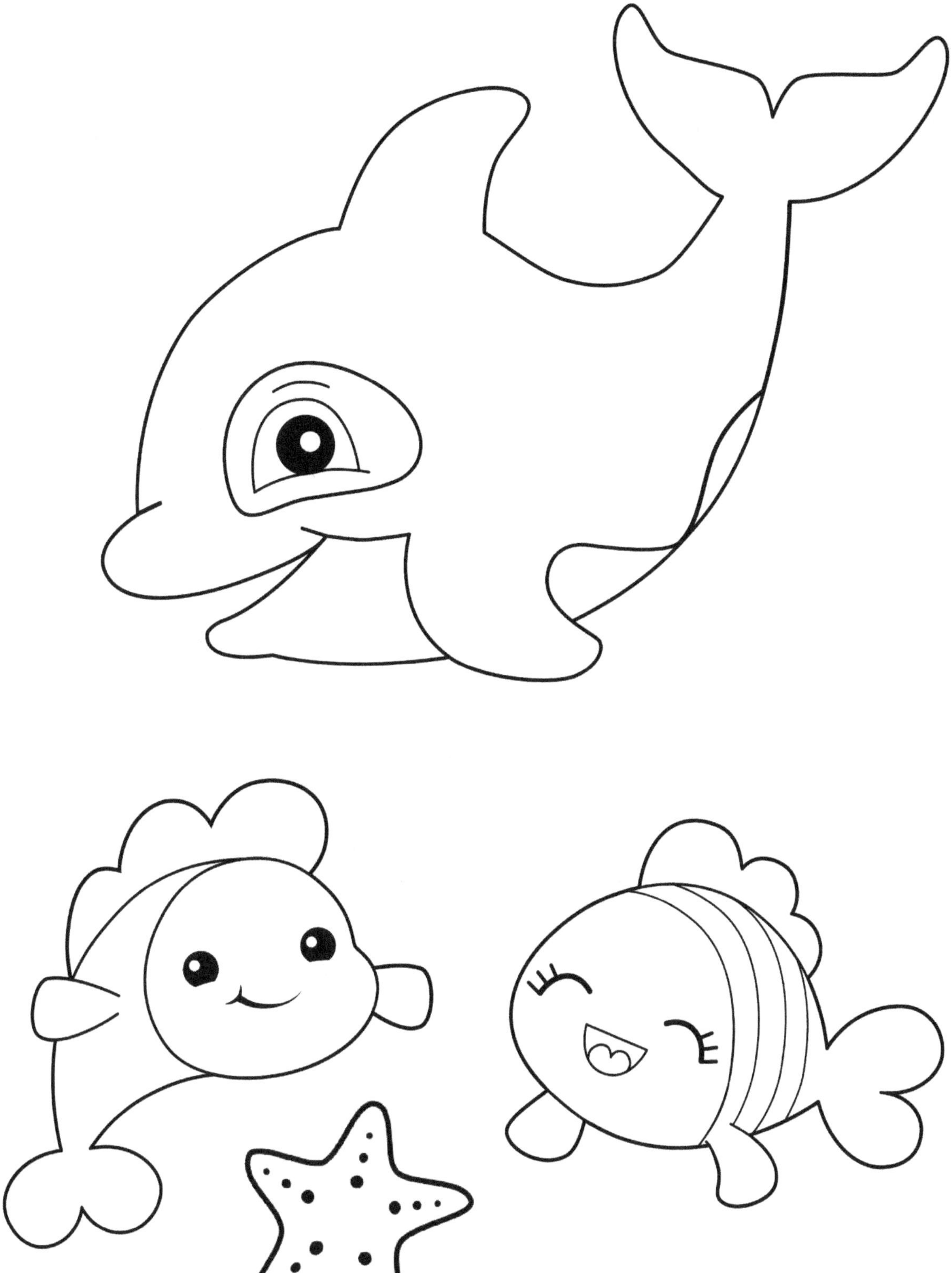

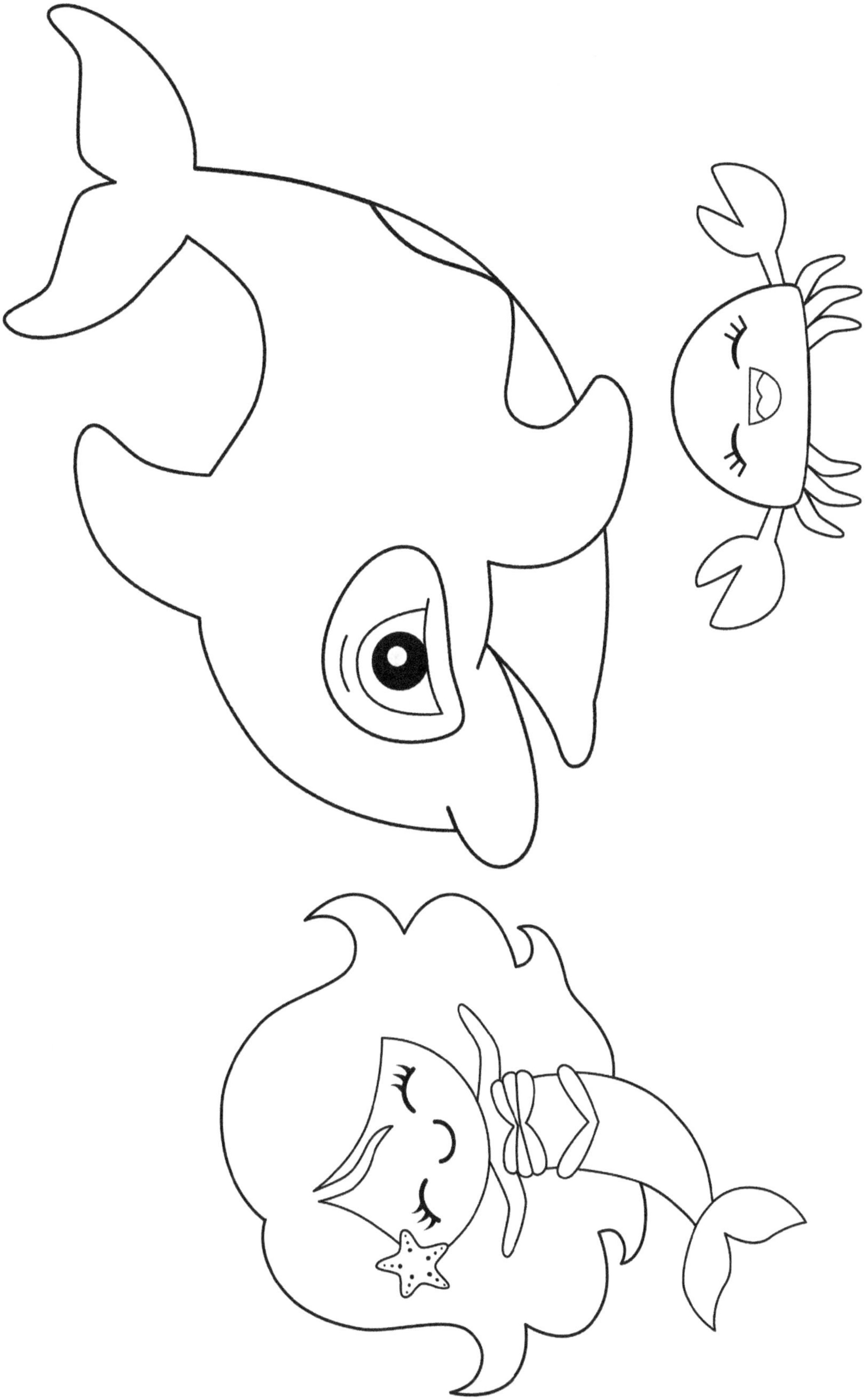

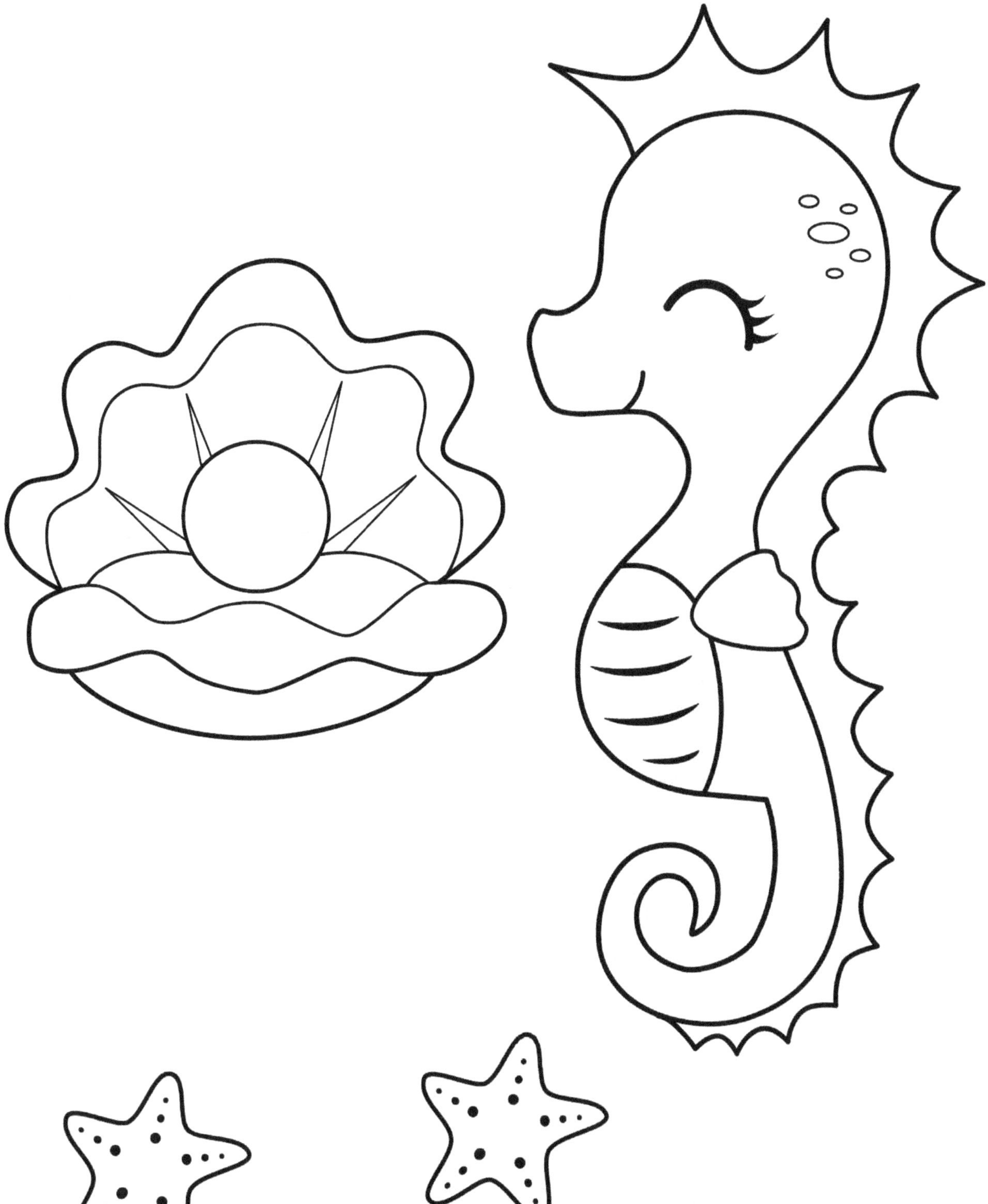

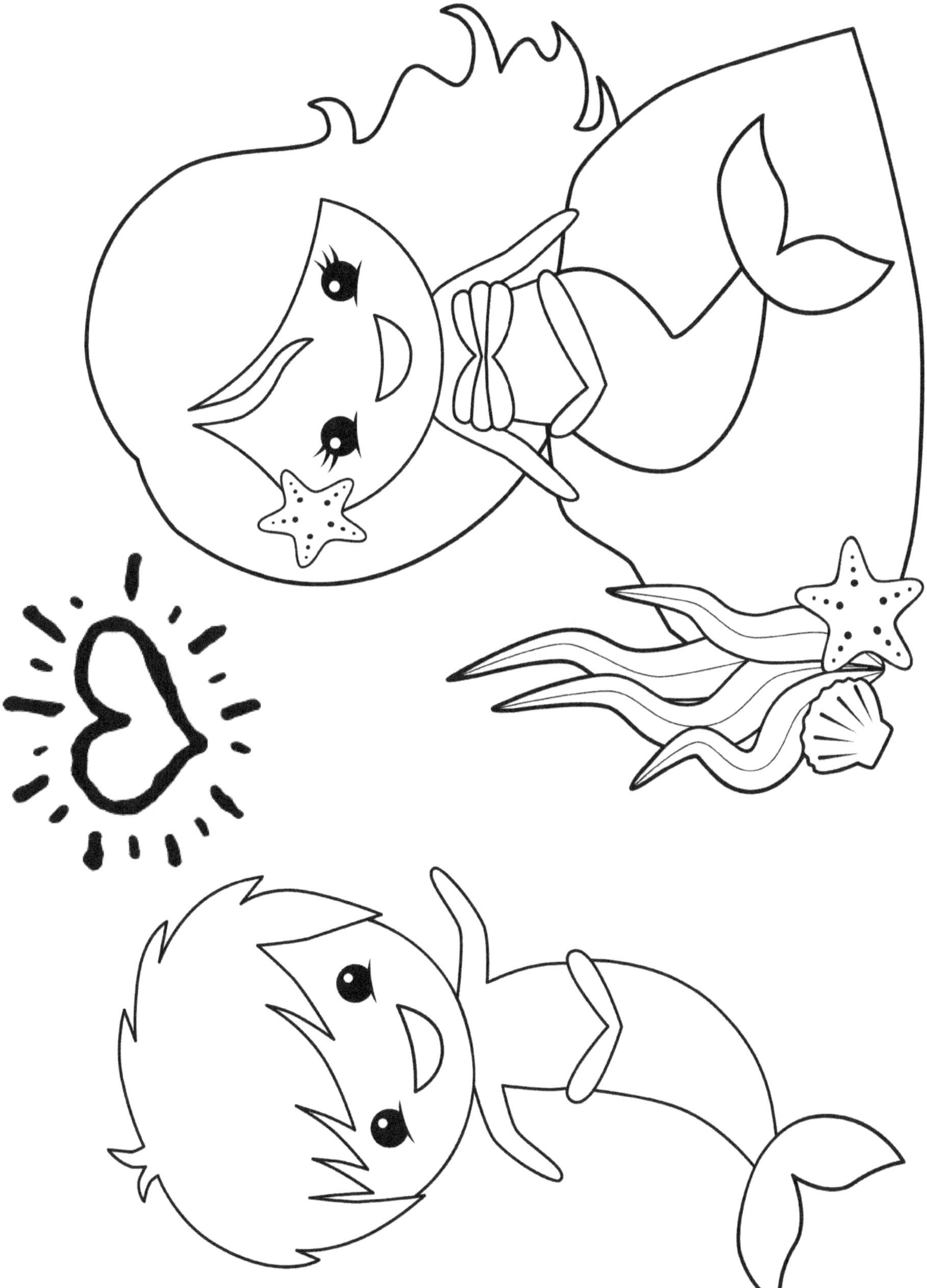

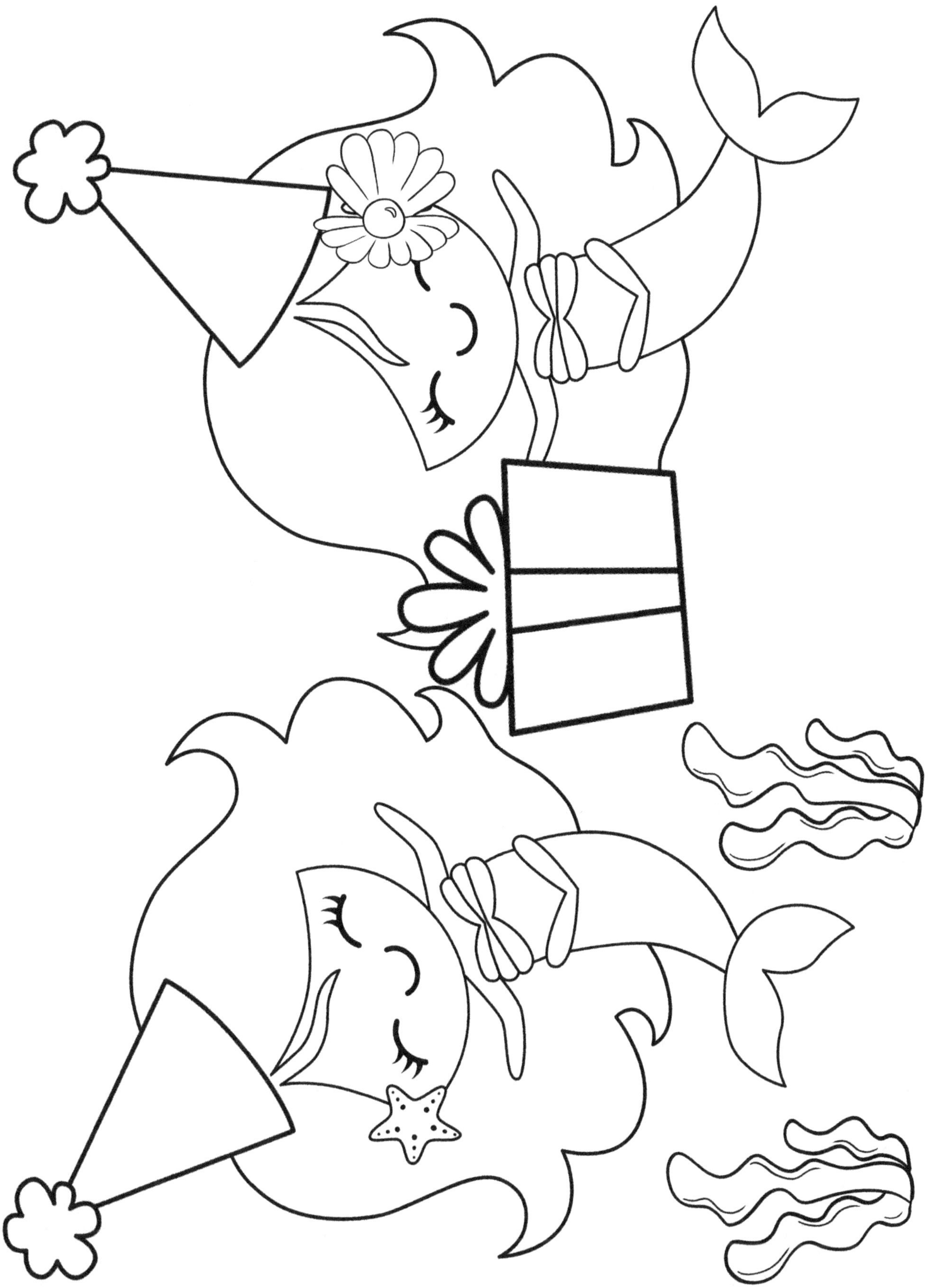

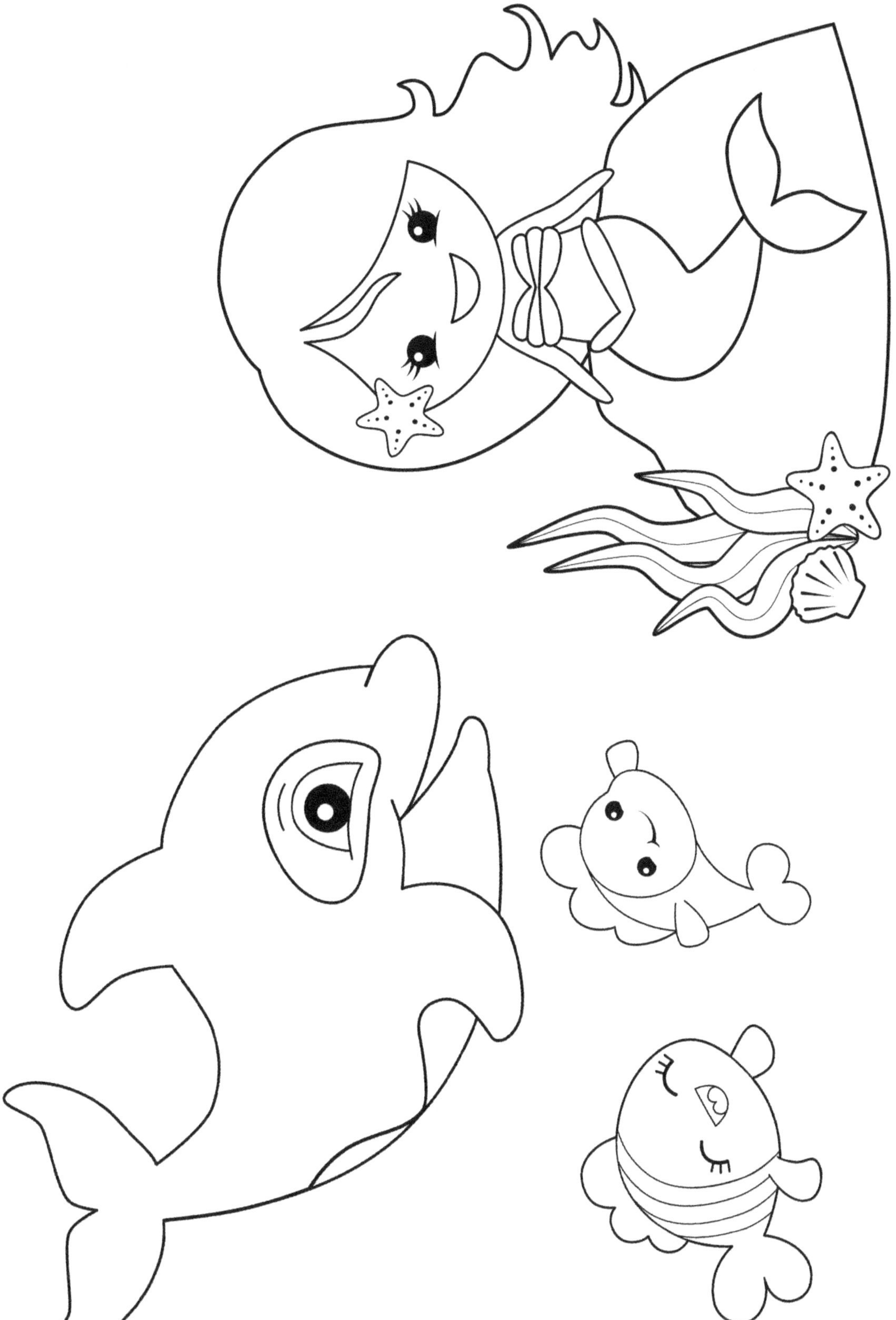

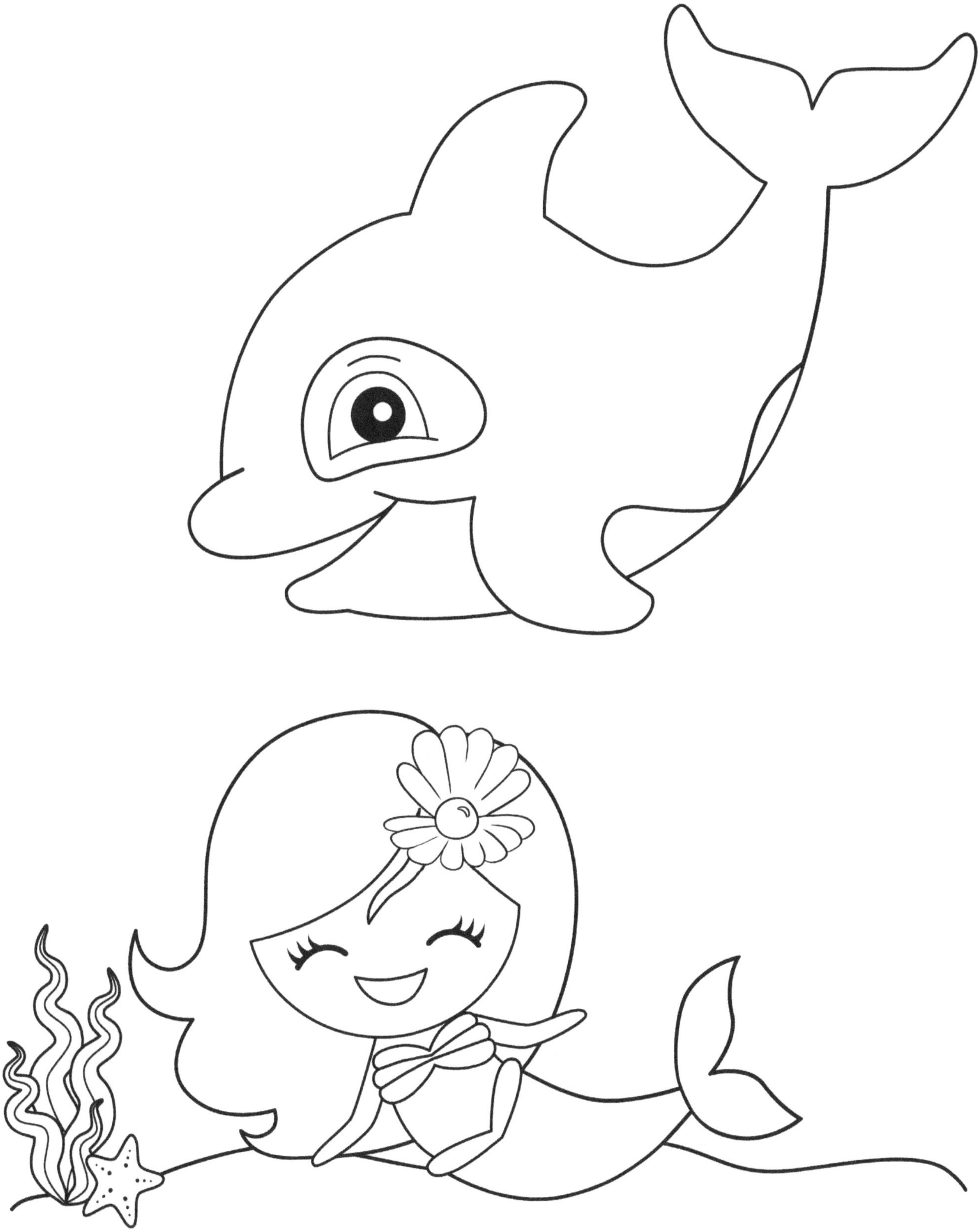

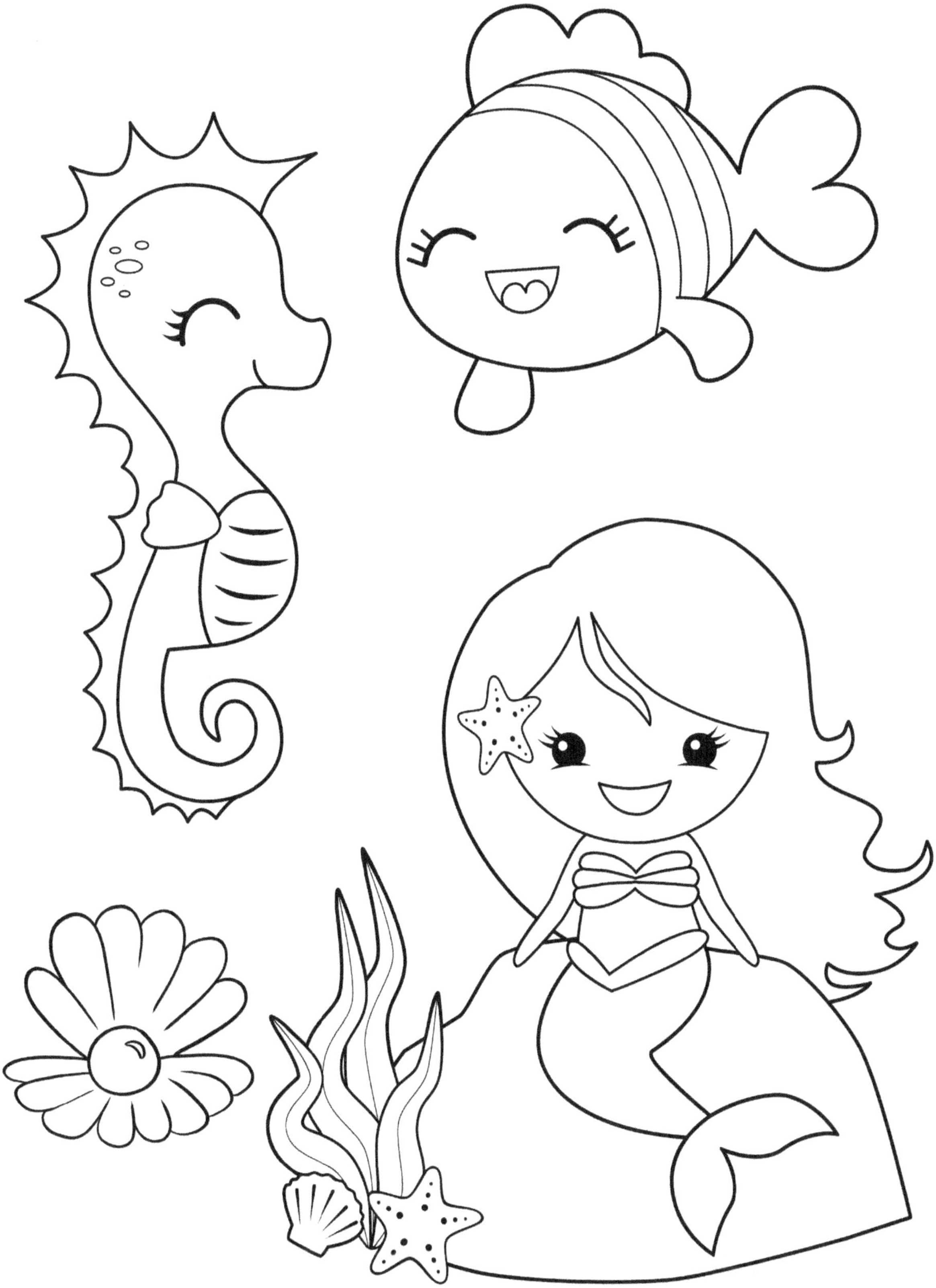

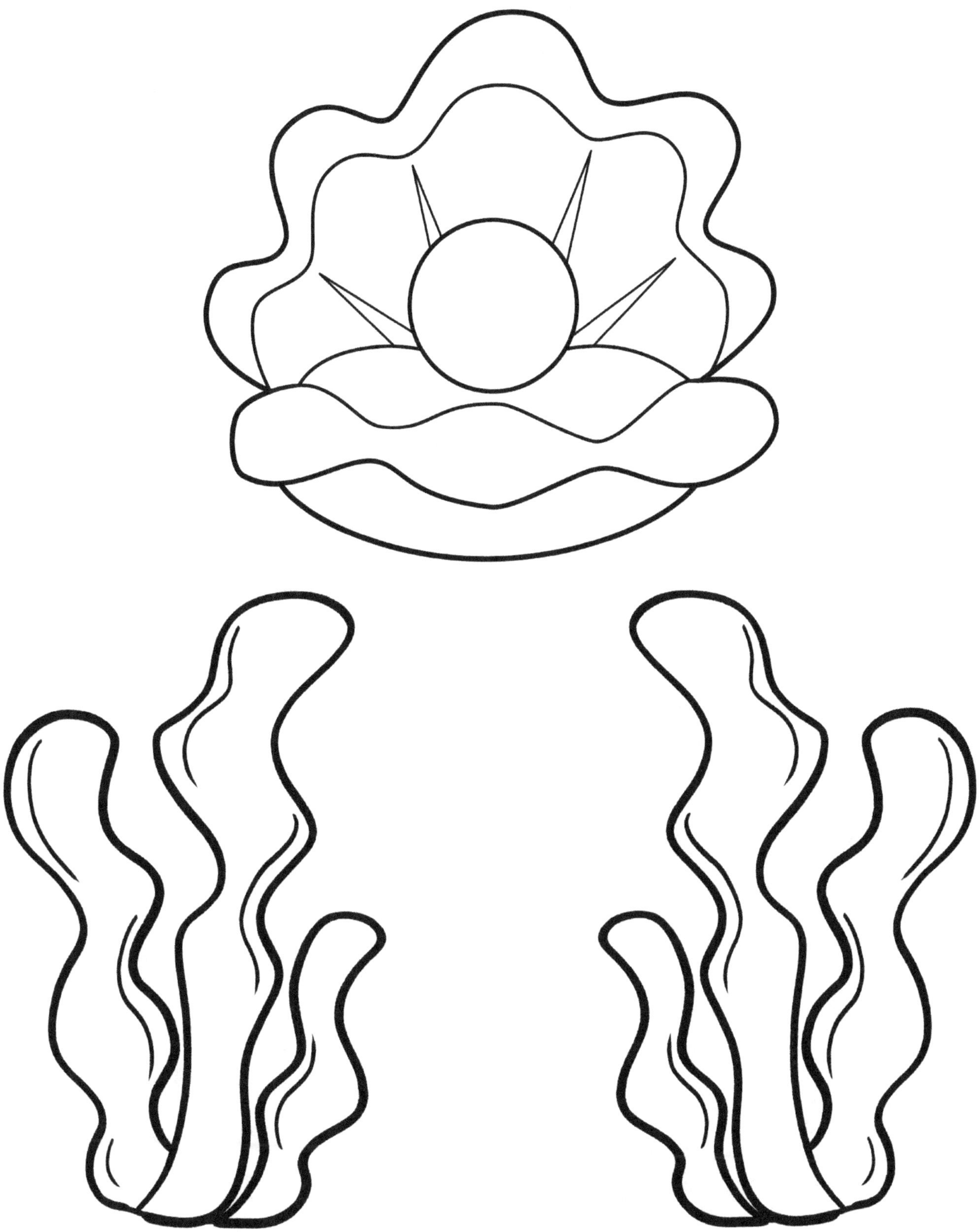

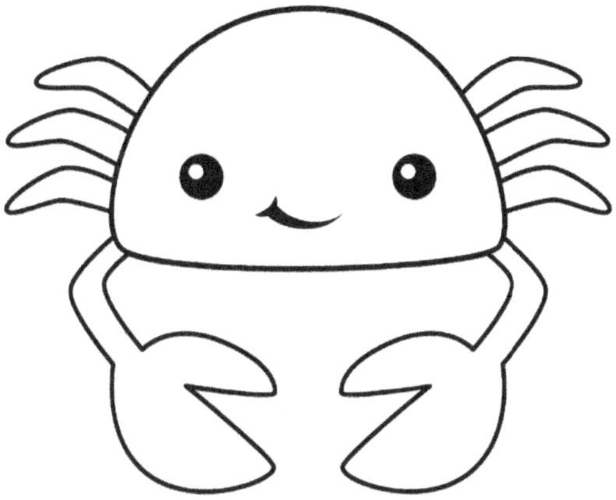
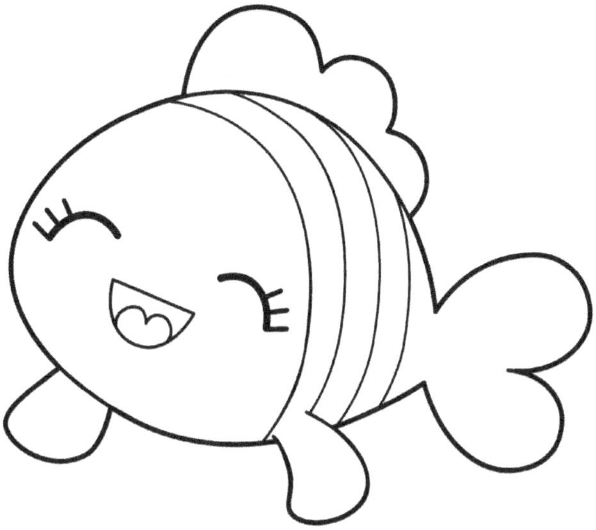
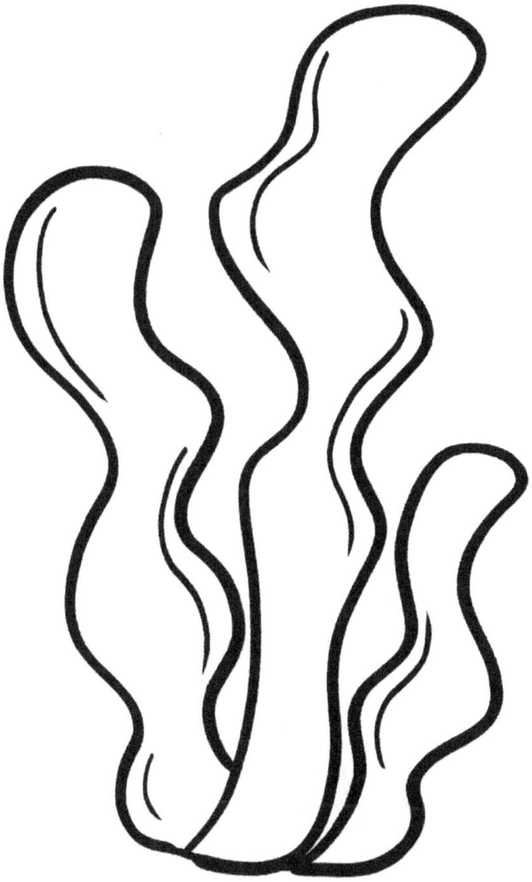
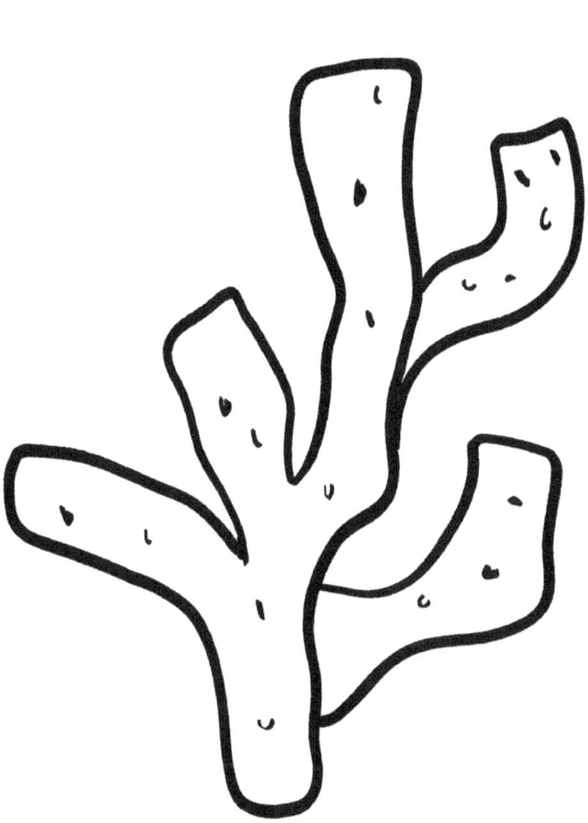

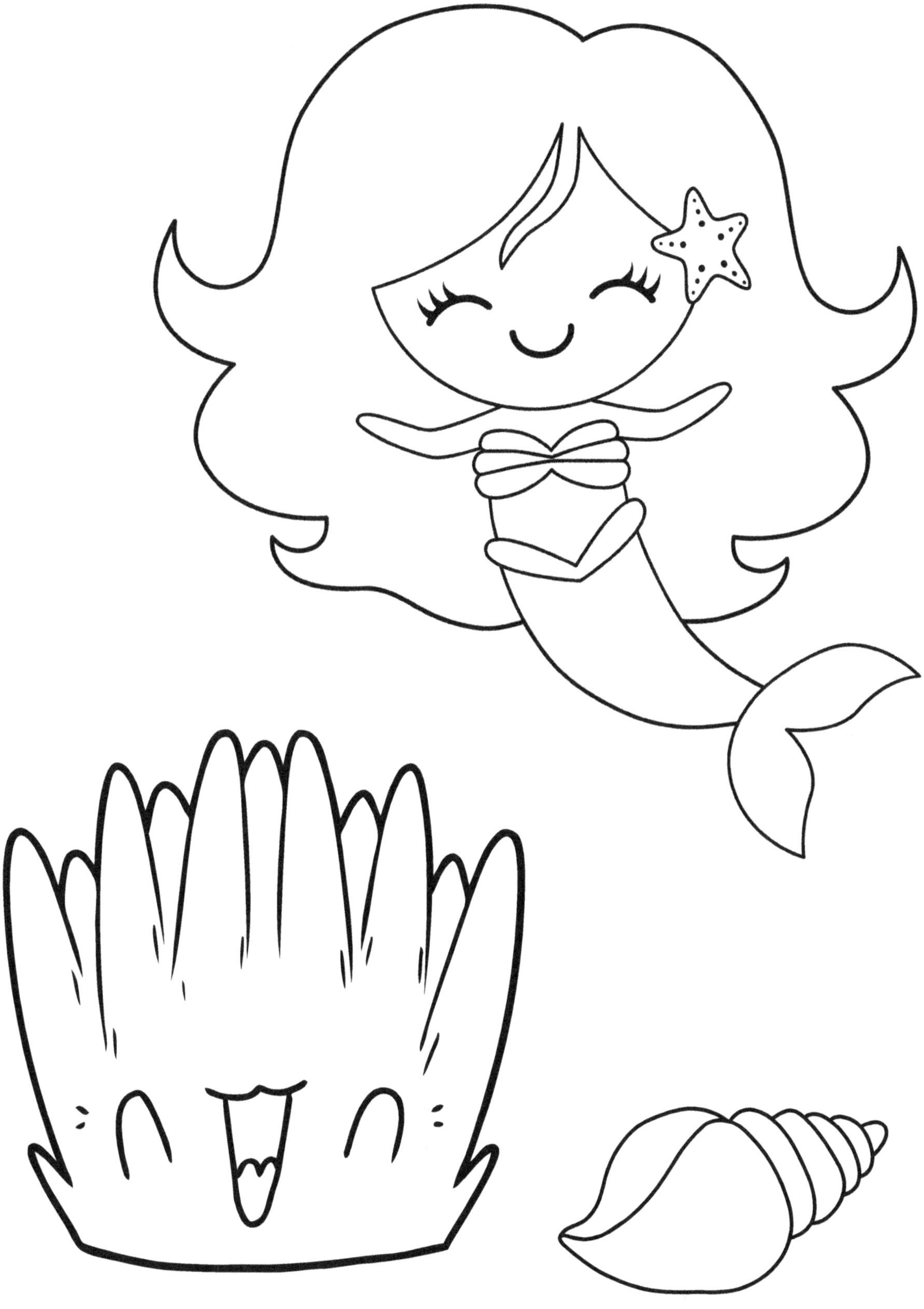

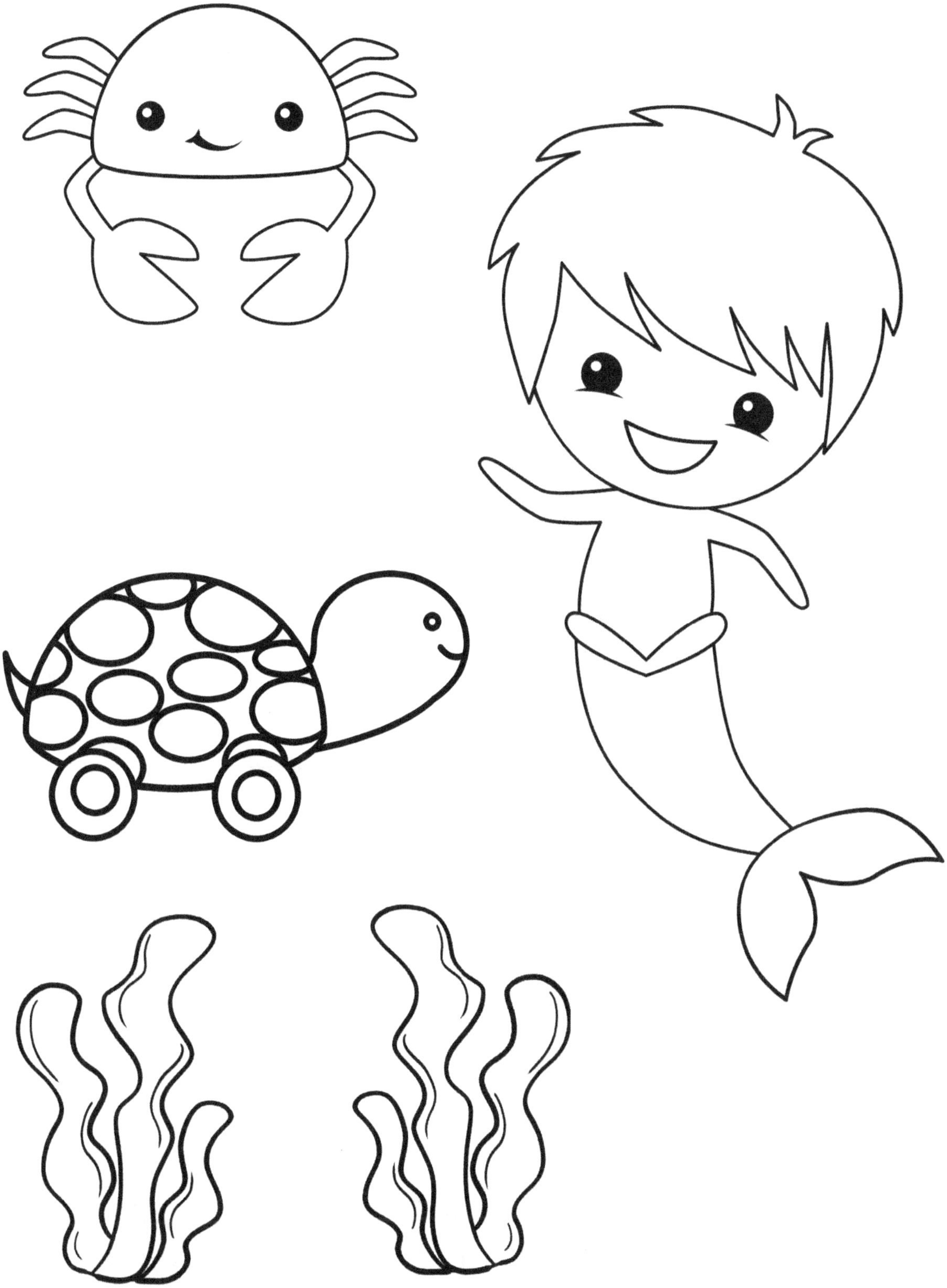

www.ingramcontent.com/pod-product-compliance
Lightning Source LLC
Chambersburg PA
CBHW080446220526
45465CB00007B/2785
9798627075211